WHY WE LOVE CATS

Other Books by Kim Levin

Why We Love Dogs

Why We Really Love Dogs

Working Dogs: Tales from Animal Planet's K-9 to 5 World

Dogs Are Funny

Dogs Love . . .

Erin Go Bark (with John O'Neill)

WHY WE LOVE CATS

A Bark & Smile™ Book

KIM LEVIN

**Andrews McMeel
Publishing**

Kansas City

03 04 05 TWP 10 9 8 7 6 5 4

ISBN: 0-7407-1864-9

Library of Congress Catalog Card Number: 2001089148

www.barkandsmile.com

For Tara, Amy, and Robin

Acknowledgments

Photographing *Why We Love Cats* was an amazing and challenging experience for me. I grew up in a household full of dogs, so my experience with cats was limited until I started photographing them a few years ago. I have always considered myself an animal lover, but I can now say that I am a true cat lover as well. I have learned why cats are so special, that you have to earn their trust and love. I have found the beauty and character that cats possess, and I hope that it shows in this book.

I want to thank John O'Neill, my husband, for his advice and guidance. I also want to thank the many generous owners who welcomed me into their homes to photograph their beloved cats. Thank you to all of the cats for teaching me to be humble and for letting me into your hearts. Special thanks to everyone at Foto Works in Red Bank, New Jersey, for their hard work developing all of the prints for this book. Thank you to Ursula Goetz, executive director of the Monmouth County SPCA, who allowed me to photograph the cats still in need of homes. Lastly, I want to thank Dorothy O'Brien, my editor, and everyone at Andrews McMeel Publishing who have provided me such a wonderful opportunity to share my photography with the public.

because they're wise

because they're fluffy

because they stop to smell the flowers

because they can squeeze into
small spaces

because they love tuna

because they're mysterious

because they're beautiful

because they long to be outside

because they're curious

because they look like lions

because they purr in our arms

because they're divas

because they were kittens once
(and some still are)

because they weave

because they find comfort anywhere

because they're lazy

because they're innocent

because they know what the other
is thinking

because they have great markings

because they yawn

because they blend right in

because they keep watch

because they share a special bond

because they're frisky

because they are not afraid
to show their emotions

because they're independent

because they love to nap

because they're agile

because they like attention

because they love Meow Mix

because they take time to get to know us,
but it's worth the wait

because they leap

because they wave to the birds

because they have their own language

because they have great balance

because they lounge

because they're sneaky

because they clean themselves . . .
all the time

"Go ahead. Make my day."

because they meow

because some of them even like dogs

because they're cute as buttons

because they have attitude

because their minds are bigger
than their mouths

because they love sitting by the window

because they beg

because they're shy

because they're peaceful

because they shake . . .

rattle . . .

and roll

because they make themselves at home

because their claws come in handy

because they dress up for Halloween

because they're finicky

because they hide

because they sun themselves

because they like their solitude

because they enjoy "the good life"

because they're unique

because they stretch . . .
like they mean it

because they have stripes

because they listen to our conversations

because they have thumbs

because they like to play

because they love the effects of catnip

because they're innocent
until proven guilty

because they love kitty condos

because they love toys

because they sit on kitchen counters

because they're cute when they wake up

because they're alert

"More milk, please."

because they burrow

because their eyes are the key
to their souls

because they have nine lives